TALES OF
PROBATION SERVICE

'It was such fun'

Edited by Jeremy Cameron & John Dessauer

With thanks to Hilary Rock

Tales of the Probation Service

Published by Stow Books

ISBN: 978-0-9548130-3-1

Printed in England by Witley Press Ltd,
24-26 Greevegate, Hunstanton, Norfolk, PE36 6AD

Other books by Jeremy Cameron:

Fiction

Vinnie Got Blown Away
It Was An Accident
Brown Bread In Wengen
Hell On Hoe St
Wider Than Walthamstow
Teenage Kicks

Non Fiction

Never Again
(A Walk From Hook of Holland to Istanbul)

Quite Quintessential
(A Walk Around the Qs)

How To Be President
(Of Norfolk Lawn Tennis Association)

Life Begins

CONTENTS

INTRODUCTION

This book is a collection of Reminiscences from people who have worked in the Probation Service. It does not represent any particular approach or view. It is geographically unbalanced and most of the contributors are not very young. We asked people if they would like to contribute some memories. Here they are.

It is still necessary to anonymise some of the contributions.

3 NELSON STREET

Ten in the morning, his usual time of arrival, Terry B in the front office, brandishing both sides of the Morning Star - the paper having been karate chopped by a fellow passenger on the top deck of the 101. His other daily reading The Racing Post was undamaged.

The front office - the size of a living room - accommodated five secretaries, a filing system and a small reception hatch. The hub of the Office, where everything was talked about, every happening reported, every tension experienced.

Terry, a martyr to the cause of the Communist Party, shrugged off suggestions he should have remonstrated with the attacker. A card carrier for many years he was hardened to expressions of disapproval; and being a believer in the good of people his passivity and willingness to forgive sometimes glowed like a gemstone. Those in his presence often glowed too.

Terry had become a Home Office mature student a couple of years earlier, retraining from a career as a craftsman brick layer. Having lived in the borough all of his life Terry talked the language, shared the beliefs, the values and the culture. Whilst not a push over, Terry had limitless tolerance and compassion. His political instincts were sharp – injustice, unfairness had to be challenged. At branch meetings he demonstrated a ring craft where idealists were encouraged to become battlers, an arena where winning mattered.

About his person would always be found a slim volume of Byron. Amongst his other heroes were Frank Sinatra and Bobby Moore. He was not averse to taking a bottle of Scotch into interviews with the more elderly of his caseload who sought chat and assurance.

This is the story of 3 Nelson Street E6: when for half a dozen years from the mid '70s the East Ham Probation Office became theatre, with Individual cameos, set pieces, farce, comedy, high drama and plenty of the absurd.

East Ham Town Hall a Grade 2 Listed Edwardian building opened in 1903. A distinct and elegant landmark, this civic complex also housed the Library, the Court House, the Swimming Pool, the Fire Station, the Social Services and, tucked away along a side street, the Probation Office.

On two floors with an attic the building could not have been less suited to the work of Probation. Rooms were either too small or too large – the waiting area was a space on the ground floor 7' by 7'. Two toilets, which supplied the only running water, no kitchen, but there was a fridge and power point in the filing room. There was no fire escape. Painted inside and out in that post war municipal green the building could have been mistaken for a public lavatory.

By the mid '70s in the belated expansion of the Service most Probation teams consisted of the well established whose training would have been variable, the new graduates with their CQSW and a sprinkling of mature entrants coming through the Home Office One Year Course. A potent mix. Nelson Street seemed often to resemble a battleground.

Of the established and experienced there were two - Barbara M and Geoff W. Both knew the locality, both were highly regarded by the Courts, and both knew how things should be done in and around the office, and moreover were unrestrained in the expression of their views.

Of the mature entrants Terry B was joined by Sandra B who similarly had strong borough links living a few streets from the office. Of the new you will be introduced to Vince W and Stuart R.

Big Barbara - an affectionate term, 6'2' and straight as a lamppost - had been a Police Officer with the Met before switching to Probation. These were the days when women Police Officers focused solely upon welfare. Barbara M had firm views about criminal justice, and she often found herself in arguments about how best erring women and children should be regarded. Another irritant for her younger colleagues concerned what they would say was a blind spot in her support of well off gangster families of which there were more than a handful. Raising money from charities for these families during the imprisonment of their bread winner was seen to be odd given that most people visiting the Office hardly had a penny to their name.

Coming out of Barbara M's office one evening a somewhat rude young man threw an insult in her direction. From a seat in the waiting area: was heard: 'Mrs M would you like me to see to it?' The words were spoken by a well-known local boxer who had become a gangster or the other way around.

Somewhat paradoxically given her generally negative beliefs about offenders Barbara M out of the blue decided to start a group for men who were chronically prone to indecently expose themselves. Within a few months there was already a waiting list and each week Barbara M would meet a dozen or so men of all ages with one thing in common – an inability to manage the desire to expose.

Re-offending rates quickly diminished. How and why Barbara M had become so successful remained a mystery because she did not adhere to any theoretical model or practice.

Each Christmas she arranged a party in the office. All of the secretaries were invited to participate suitably frocked. These dreaded occasions were heart-warming once this group of shy, socially inept men were forced on to their feet to dance. By the end inhibitions had disappeared and haunted looks turned to laughter and smiles.

If this had ended here Barbara M might have avoided the notoriety that was to follow. Details of this unusual project attracted attention. Barbara M was interviewed for the World at One, the BBC flagship news programme of the time. Thereafter she would be frequently interviewed for publications from around the world.

The Chief became very concerned because he had heard her give a talk to magistrates and was convinced she did not know what she was doing. Eventually a rogue journalist from the Catholic Herald approached the News of the World. On the Friday before Sunday publication the Chief had a long row with the Editor - nothing new in that because the Chief relished every opportunity for a row. On the Sunday front page was a large picture of Barbara M under the heading 'SEXPERT'.

Sandra B a nervous quiet young woman would not see herself as being a character; indeed she was mostly intent on hiding away. Beneath the façade of shyness was to be found a rebellious nature combined with a cantankerousness which produced in colleagues a frustration they sometimes could not control.

Always slow – from walking to talking to completing reports to turning up in Court. Having been allocated a Divorce Court Welfare report to prepare she discovered that the disputing couple knew a thing or two about children. The father was a Director of Social Services and the mother a journalist on a national newspaper. Sandra B set about the work with all of her customary pedestrian planning. Soon both parties were attacking her for her delays, her perceived obstinacy and her diligence. Before deciding she should make way for a more experienced colleague the mother had told her that the father was allegedly having an affair with Sandra B's ACO (Assistant Chief Officer)!

Enter stage left Geoff W. Geoff W would best be described as being a PO of the old school. One morning a week he would walk around what he called his patch, in Manor Park. Here he would be on the look out for nefarious activity from either present or previous members of his caseload. He had an extensive knowledge of people and families, and as he would put it 'knew what they were up to'. Whilst there were occasional glimpses of paranoia Geoff W was regarded as being simply unusual. A NAPO Rule Book pedant he gained the reputation of being a serial irritant of management.

Geoff W took over the welfare report from Sandra B and immediately explored the possibility the ACO might be influencing the legal process because of her supposed association with one of the parties. The ACO was encouraged to meet with Geoff W to clear up any misunderstanding or confusion. Whilst the meeting was said to have been agreeable what happened next was most disagreeable. Unbeknown to the ACO the meeting had been secretly recorded by Geoff W who then saw fit to share the contents with the mother's lawyer. The expression 'all hell broke loose' is a reasonable description of what followed.

Geoff W was suspended and within a week had handed in his notice claiming harassment. The leaving party took place in the Court and was attended by at least 75 magistrates, who could not understand why their model and darling probation officer was being allowed to go! Geoff W characteristically knew the rules about constructive dismissal. In the week before the Employment Tribunal hearing many months later there was frantic activity by management aiming desperately to avoid damaging publicity and at the last moment Geoff W accepted a deal including a reference. Geoff W went to work in Holland as a PO, wrote a book on criminology and got married.

Arguments, rumours, sub texts, comedy. What more might you want from a day at the office?

Waiting in the wings is Stuart R. Graduate entrant, fierce intelligence, argumentative and prone to outbreaks of impetuous behaviour. Large in frame with a bulky appearance Stuart R would often find his body out of synch with his considerable brain.

The pantomime antics as he sought to extricate himself from each physical disaster were entertaining but were nothing when compared with the scrapes he got into with clients and families. Stuart R certainly represented the new in Nelson Street. Reports were lengthy and detailed. He worked with and most importantly engaged closely with the most challenging of clients.

One mid-morning there was shouting and commotion in the office with everyone running outside to see Stuart R grappling on the roof with a client who had broken off from their chat deciding to leave prematurely by the upstairs window. Order was restored, but disorder reprised a few weeks later with a different client. Stuart R had persuaded the Police to assist with a journey for medical intervention. This time the client attempted to escape from a moving vehicle. Those in the office called to the scene in the High Road talked of seeing Stuart R haplessly wrestling in the road, shirt ripped from his shoulder.

Police and sightseers looked on - shocked, entertained, bewildered. Order was restored.

The final piece of action was neither pantomime, farce nor comedy. Around midday on the last day of the working week Stuart R burst into the front office carrying the smallest of babies. He explained that during a home visit he had been so concerned for the safety of the infant he considered instant removal was needed. Whilst everyone scurried to find procedures for this sort of thing Barbara M was making a similar home visit to the same family. Returning sharply to Nelson Street, with gusto she reported the stealing of a baby.

Two POs were working with the same family but neither had knowledge of their mutual interest. The ensuing complaint was whitewashed, but what had always been an uneasy relationship between the established PO and the new generation PO did not improve.

Eventually Stuart R went off to become an SPO in a West Country prison –'somewhere perhaps I can do less damage'.

Inevitably there will be a Priest in the cast. Vince W spent 4 years in a seminary before becoming a gravedigger and then becoming a probation officer. Vince W spent a lifetime questioning his beliefs, questioning his abilities and questioning everyone else about why they tolerated or colluded with social injustice. To use one of his favourite words 'disabuse'

11

please do not think that this young man was without wit or humour – he could bring people to their knees with a chance observation or an apt phrase.. Vince W was revered far and wide by his vast clientele, and when he did not infuriate them, by his peers.

As with those outfits that chased fires for insurance money, Vince W had an addiction for a crisis. The attraction never became clear, but the consequences were manifest. Whatever was on the stocks at the time was quickly discarded whilst he raced to the next big event. The problem here was that half written reports were never completed and records were rarely given the time of day. Against this background had to be factored in what Vince W described as a genetic predisposition to do everything to perfection.

Long, detailed Crown Court reports were delivered breathlessly by hand whilst the Judges twiddled their fingers. Working in the office throughout the night in preparation for an inspection, establishing a caseload or rather a flock of the most deprived and troubled people in the borough, creating frustration - no, fury - amongst colleagues whenever deadlines were missed - but there was something else. Compared with all of the other members of the cast Vince W was the only true anarchist. Any order or instruction would be subtly defied if he disagreed or believed it unfair. Paradoxically whilst he was clearly unmanageable his various managers over the years offered him unconditional protection. Several times whilst in

Nelson Street during this time he offered to hand in his notice because of yet another disastrous procrastination. Each time it was ignored.

Given his first Divorce Court Welfare Report to prepare Vince W after 6 months offered an interim submission – it ran to 50 pages. On being asked to explain Vince W simply said that he was working on having the couple reconcile!

The final scene involves the theft of his beloved battered Mk 1 Cortina. With his brother he scoured the borough and on a Sunday afternoon in neighbouring Barking came across the vehicle. Vince W explained that he simply stole it back. No police or any of that sort of stuff. 'If anyone was so desperate to take this car they would not need any more aggravation.'

Wherever he went after leaving Nelson Street the pattern remained of gathering a flock, looking after people rather than looking after himself. Even in the months before his premature death Vince W was running a soup kitchen and generally tending to the homeless. Character or saint?

. The front office was the scene of carbon paper and late reports and POs offloading their most recent accounts of awfulness. One Monday evening someone entered from the waiting area and grabbed a large handful of the card index system. The theft was not discovered until later in the evening when members of the public finding the scattered cards in nearby Central Park responsibly took them to the Police Station. The following day the Chief had to draft a reply to the Home Secretary who had been asked to respond to a question in the House. The Chief warmed to any opportunity to remind the Government of its neglect of the Probation Service and its staff.

This was the room when every Friday at 11am the hatch would be opened to a man of unknown identity who would provide a burst of the trumpet and then retreat.

On Friday afternoon Terry B argued that if the building trade stopped work and went to the pub why shouldn't Probation? So he was never alone in the Denmark Arms and when the pub chucked out at 3.30 pm he and whoever had accompanied him would in relaxed mood return to enliven the office.

At 4pm now and the work of the week was coming to a close, the office was strangely at peace and people are drifting away.

As the curtain comes down Terry B will be heard crooning the Sinatra songbook.

Oh such wonderful days.

Mike Head

THE MODERN WAY
(On Privatisation)

We were told that we would have to attend meetings first thing every morning - and we would have to stand up whilst being 'talked at'.

However, after a lot of opposition it was decided we were able to sit....

These sessions continued for a few weeks.

Then one of our more enthusiastic managers hit on the idea of having a 'word for the day' suggestion at the beginning of the meeting to get us in the right mood. This was feeling more and more like an American car company cheerleader exercise.

We racked our brains to come up with something not too hostile - and on this particular morning I proffered 'deluded'.

I add that these sessions were to 'aim for gold' in order to privatise the Probation Service.

They got what they deserved.

Jackie Foot

1972....

In 1972 as a young probation officer in a north London suburb I found in my in tray a Social Enquiry Report request for me to complete on a Mr. Bruce (not his real name). Mr. Bruce had appeared at the local Magistrates Court having pleaded guilty to assault section 47. The circumstances were that he had jumped the queue at the DHSS office and when told to return to his place in the queue had thrown a telephone at the DHSS officer.

It seemed straight forward enough. I wrote to Mr. Bruce with a date and time when I would visit him at his home in order to prepare the report. In those days there were no health and safety guidelines.

On the day in question I turned up at the defendant's door to be greeted by his mother, a little old lady. I explained my visit and she looked worried. 'Alfie's not himself today,' she said.

In my ignorance I assured her that all would be well. If there was a problem then I was sure I could help him overcome it. "Advise, Assist and Befriend".

Our discussion was interrupted by a heavy footfall on the stairs, as Alfred Bruce descended from the floor above. He was a man in his early fifties, stocky but powerfully built. I introduced myself as his mother invited me to take a seat.

Mr. Bruce, however, continued to pace the floor. I explained the purpose of my visit and said that I hoped my report would help him when he appeared in court. (Those were the days when that was the purpose of such reports). Mr. Bruce brightened. 'That's right,' he said, 'I do need help'. I thought things were going well. Then he launched himself across the room and had me by the throat, beginning to throttle me as he bellowed, 'I need help'.

I was seated in a large easy chair that had seen better days. Both the springs and the cushions were shot and I sank, unable to regain my feet as Mr. Bruce throttled me while bellowing his need for help. 'Leave the gentleman alone,' his mother cried timidly, 'I understand how you feel,' I croaked.

Then, with the superhuman strength one finds on such occasions, I managed to lurch to my feet. We reeled about the room, he still grasping my throat while I endeavoured to kick his feet from under him. By a lucky chance I succeeded and we fell heavily to the floor. His breath was knocked from him, his grip on my throat loosened and I was able to stand and get a table between us. He hesitated then said, 'I'm sorry, shouldn't have done that'. Reassured, I began to utter soothing words when with a roar he launched himself at me once more. This time I fled out the door to my car and sped off.

Attempting to grasp the situation I became concerned for Mr. Bruce's mother. Was she safe alone with this violent man? I returned to the office but it was late. The only person there was my senior, Peter, a World War II fighter ace. Who better to deal with the situation?

We agreed I should phone the after-hours local authority social worker. I did this and alerted him to our concerns for the mother. His response took me aback. 'Oh, we never go to that address,' he said. 'He's far too violent.'

Next day in the office tea room I told my story to my colleagues, who were agog. Then in the midst of my tale the receptionist poked her head round the door and said that there was a Mr. Bruce to see me. Suddenly my colleagues all found better things to do.

But Peter, to his eternal credit, came with me to the waiting room. As soon as he saw us, Mr. Bruce leapt at us, arms outstretched, ranting and roaring. We fled into the receptionist's room, locked the door and phoned the adjoining court police team. The thud of heavy boots alerted Mr. Bruce to the arrival of six of London's finest. He responded by falling to the floor and lying prone and still. The police immediately became sympathetic towards him and suspicious of Peter and me and our actions. 'Here, what have you done to the poor fellah?' they demanded of us.

We jump forward several weeks to the local Magistrates' Court and the adjourned hearing. My report contained the events of that fateful evening and also Mr. Bruce's history which I had obtained from Social Services. He had been involved in the Second World War battle for Monte Cassino in Italy where he had been blown up and shell shocked. He had never been able to move on from that terrible experience and repeatedly re-lived its horrors.

The police, still sympathetic, allowed him to sit with his mum in the body of the court. He sat there looking as though butter would not melt in his mouth. The magistrates read my report and clearly could not reconcile my account with the smiling, seemingly mild mannered individual they saw in front of them. Uncertain what to do, and after considerable deliberations, they remanded him once more, this time for a psychiatric report - but in custody.

When Mr. Bruce heard this he launched a repeat of the battle for Monte Cassino. Chairs, court furniture and police officers went flying. Eventually he was manhandled to the cells while I reflected that at the very least my report might now be taken a little more seriously.

When the case returned to court the psychiatric report advocated that he be sectioned and this was duly done. Two weeks later there was a sequel. I was driving down the high street and there was Mr. Bruce, oblivious of the traffic, rampaging and roaring down the centre of the road. Too much for the psychiatric hospital, they had released him with their blessing and little else.

Several months later I had a new senior, a young man intent on going places. Unlike Peter, the fighter ace, he did not believe it was his role to support his officers. He allocated me a fresh report on Mr. Bruce, who had been arrested on new charges.

I hurried to explain the history and suggested we explain to the court why the preparation of a fresh report appeared both undesirable and dangerous. The new senior thought differently. Someone has to do it and it might as well be you, was his attitude. I suspected he thought a refusal might reflect badly on his career.

I brooded on what to do and stupidly decided I would show him. I would do the report. I should have taken the matter to a higher authority or involved NAPO, but these were times when you didn't do such things. So I went to see Mr. Bruce and interviewed him on his doorstep and at arm's length. It was possibly the worst report I have ever written. However, it was never presented as he didn't turn up at court and neither the court nor the police seemed anxious to find him,

Several years later I had moved on when I heard that Mr. Bruce was involved in a final tragic episode. I was told that he had attacked his GP and blinded him. Once more he had been placed in a psychiatric hospital but this time seemingly never to be released.

John Dessauer

A SCAPEGOATING INCIDENT

At the time when London Probation Service stopped its officers undertaking prison visits outside the M25, I was supervising a prisoner outside this catchment area. The prisoner's parole hearing was taking place and required the probation officer's attendance.

I was working at the Public Protection Unit and my police colleagues there, learning that no probation officer should drive to prisons outside the M25, offered to take me in a police vehicle to attend the hearing. This option was put to the senior probation officer but was turned down under the no visit policy.

The prisoner contacted the Probation Ombudsman, stating that because of the failure of the probation officer to attend, his case had suffered and he was still in prison.

The Ombudsman interviewed me, the Senior and the Assistant Chief Officer. The SPO and the ACO cooperated to lay the blame on me, as I had seemingly failed to make a case for the visit. They also went about changing all the Delius record of contacts describing discussions with the prisoner, police etc. The investigation concluded that the SPO and ACO contended it was my failure in not making a special case which culminated in my not attending the Parole Board hearing. The two managers basically decided to lay the blame on me.

Anon

ALL RISE

Ethel was a very, very regular attender at court. Of diminutive stature and with a face made for gurning, she was a chronic alcoholic. When drunk she was formidable, a force to be reckoned with, possessed of a tongue and turn of language that was more than a match for anyone.

The first time I recall seeing her she was entering the court building, pausing only to pluck a cigarette from the mouth of an astonished passer-by. Transferring the cigarette to her own mouth she entered the court.

Let us pass over the uproar when she waltzed into the court, fag dangling from her lips. Magistrates, clerks and ushers, incensed at her behaviour, bawled and shouted. Ethel, revelling in the scene she was creating, shouted out mock apologies while in an elaborate pantomime stamping out the offending ciggy.

What followed was even more extraordinary. The charge when put was: "Criminal Damage to a Dead Body".

No one had heard of such a thing. Ethel was represented by an unfortunate and despairing duty solicitor who assisted her to enter an incoherent not guilty plea.

The prosecution case was surprisingly straightforward. Ethel had run into an undertaker's in the mistaken belief that she was being chased by... someone. Dashing into the chapel she had knocked a coffin from its trestle, causing the deceased to tumble out on to the floor. It created, as the prosecution put it, 'considerable distress'. The defence case was also straightforward. Ethel thought she was being pursued by a man she did not know and could not identify. Others present, however, were unanimous in agreeing that there was no such pursuer.

The magistrates had no hesitation in returning a guilty verdict. But more was to follow. A quite separate offence was to be taken into consideration. It was a theft charge, a shop lifting offence involving the theft from a shoe shop of two shoes, both for the left foot.

The magistrates, long accustomed to Ethel's antics, felt they had on this occasion no alternative but to pass a sentence of six months imprisonment. But only for the coffin offence. With a sigh, they passed no sentence for the two left shoes. So Ethel was taken away to Holloway, which, as she had endured many similar sentences, held no fears for her.

Another court appearance for Ethel was preceded by a visit to the probation office. Such visits were not uncommon as she used our office to resolve many and various problems. On this occasion she arrived clutching a half empty bottle of vodka and in a tipsy state, to seek the assistance of the duty officer, Ian. Her problem, she explained, was that she had run out of colostomy bags, now known as stoma bags. Now this was no responsibility of ours but Ian recognised Ethel's inability to manage her own affairs so he sat her down in the waiting room while he visited a chemist and purchased the necessary bags. We had a befriending fund for just such occasions.

Several weeks passed and then Ethel appeared back in court on some trifling charge or other. She pleaded guilty to the charge and the unfortunate duty solicitor launched into whatever mitigation he could advance. Mary became bored with proceedings and her gaze wandered the court. Suddenly her eyes fixed on the probation bench where sat the duty PO, Ian.

'Here,' shouted Ethel, bringing the proceedings to a halt. 'Here, there's the probation officer who bought me my colostomy bags.' All eyes turned on Ian and silence fell. It was broken once more by Ethel. 'Wrong size,' she concluded. Perhaps her contribution helped obtain the subsequent Conditional Discharge.

Then there was the occasion not at court but at the local hospital, although the occasion still featured the probation office. Ethel was due to have an operation but the hospital recognised that her alcoholism and a chronic fear of hospitals were likely to cause real problems. So they contacted the Probation Service for assistance.

Now Ethel, through her many appearances at court, had built a good relationship with me, so it was agreed that I should be with her as she was taken to the operating theatre, in the hope that this would have a calming influence. On the day in question I went to the ward where Ethel was being prepared for surgery, only to come upon an extraordinary sight.

There was Ethel, clad in a NHS robe, wrestling on the floor with the surgeon while several nurses made ineffectual efforts to separate them. 'Let me go,' shouted Ethel. 'Save me, please save me,' cried the surgeon. 'Send for security,' bawled the nurses.

Ethel broke free and, with a surprising turn of speed, headed down the corridor, NHS robe trailing behind her, hotly pursued by the surgeon, the nurses and me. It was a scene reminiscent of a Benny Hill sketch or a Carry On film. Out the exit she flew and once in the hospital grounds she quickly lost the pursuing group who returned to the hospital, the operation postponed to another day.

The strangest twist of all occurred when the Probation Service formed a group with a local doctor to cater for the needs of those with alcohol problems. With no great hope Ethel was enrolled and within a relatively short time a transformation occurred. She stopped drinking and her behaviour became exemplary. Indeed, at one meeting of the group some visiting magistrates mistook her for one of their number, so very correct was her demeanour. This miraculous change lasted for several months, then some inevitable crisis saw her slide off the wagon once more and the old Ethel returned. She continued to attend the group but its reforming abilities for her were sadly spent.

As time passed, her appearances at court diminished and then ceased. I shall never forget her as she was, nor shall I forget the other cast of characters who over the years passed before the court. All human life was there.

Marie Clarke

GLORY DAYS

There was a time when NAPO – and NAPO AGM – was a force to be reckoned with. I know that nostalgia isn't what it used to be, but I am saddened and angry at our loss of a voice to be heard. Remember AGM 2005?

The merger of prisons and probation had taken place in 2003 with the creation of NOMS (National Offender Management Service). Martin Narey, previous SPAD (special adviser) to Michael Gove, was CE of NOMS from 2004. The NAPO Action Group publication Probe 2004 led with a superbly written, coruscating article "No to NOMS" by Alison Barkley (see excerpt below).

By the 2005 AGM Martin Narey had cleared off to Barnardo's. Despite his departure NAPO HQ invited him to speak at AGM. Alison, on behalf of NAPO Action, proposed an emergency motion saying we had more important things to discuss than listening to someone who hadn't even bothered to stick around (no doubt realising the debacle that was NOMS but not prepared to criticise publicly).

The motion was overwhelmingly passed. Apparently Narey was actually en route when he got the telephone call to say AGM didn't want him. He had to turn around and go home.

2004 Alison Barkley writing in Probe:

"Are you angry? I'm absolutely, incandescently, vituperatively, furiously angry at this slash and burn approach to probation – we have been rubbished and shat upon for far too long

We do not need to be diverted into time-consuming, spurious and flawed data collection (e.g. Oasys) with the illusion that this achieves anything at all. We should resist the tick box approach in court reports. We do not need ludicrous targets corrupting our Practice. We are not a manufacturing industry. We should be very angry at the deprofessionalisation of our work.

We do need to promote the work of constructive relationship building with our clients. Most people come to us with damaged lives and turning this around is what we do. With sensible resourcing and provision of the right type of supporting services, we could achieve massive results.

Be confident in what we are about.

Unite and fight."

It is fitting to remember this in fond memory of Alison who died in August 2018.

Judy Green

HOME VISIT

'Have you seen it?' they asked at the local nick, which I regularly visited in search of tea and gossip.

'Seen what?'

'Igor's act. We know you know him 'cos we've seen you going in his flat.'

'Well, I might know him,' I said, maintaining confidentiality at all times. I knew just what they were talking about but had never witnessed a performance and didn't want to.

Unfortunately, fate had been tempted. On my next visit he offered to demonstrate.

I tried the usual evasive tactics - staring unbelievingly at my watch and crying 'My God, is that the time?' - while darting towards the door. But I was stopped in my tracks by something I had never noticed before: the door held a pattern of deep gashes showing the unmistakeable outline of a human body.

My first thought was that the landlord would be unimpressed. But then he might not argue persuasively with a knife thrower.

My thoughts were interrupted by someone saying 'Would you mind moving over there - this is where I stand.' Whereupon a slim woman positioned herself with her back right up against the door. Was she going to get even slimmer? Then Igor stood about ten feet from her.

He must have left the room for a few moments because he was now wearing an enormous headdress. I remembered something else. Igor was partially sighted, which did not lend itself to the fine motor skills that appeared to be required. I also recalled that the partial sight was limited to one eye; he had no vision at all in the other.

It didn't look well, but short of leaping out of the (third floor) window it would be hard to escape. I was giving some thought to how I could convincingly fabricate my witness statement for the inquest when a boy of about ten also walked over to the door.

It was going to be a massacre.

However, the boy stood to one side of the target and nodded to his dad.

'Get the knives,' said Igor.

Another child appeared and produced what looked like a roll of carpet. He laid it on the floor to reveal at least half a dozen knives. Or rather machetes, at least a foot and a half long, pointed and twinkling in the half light.

Needless to say, Igor had to demonstrate their sharpness by cutting a piece from his hair with one, mercifully well-aimed stroke. Then he launched the first of the knives, which rotated surprisingly in the air with an ominous whistling sound.

When I peeped again from between my fingers, no blood was on the walls and no crumpled little figure lay on the floor. The ten year old was actually holding the knife in his gloved hand and by the handle too. Before I could speak, another knife hurtled across the room and was also caught in full flight just before it struck - and another and another, each one grasped at the last moment .

What could I say?

Fortunately those years of training and long professional experience came, as ever, to my aid. Enhancing my client's self-image, I applauded. Turning what could have been a tricky ethical challenge to my advantage, I slipped perfectly into role. 'Well,' I said, 'perhaps we could add that to your CV. Speaking of which, the Job Centre tell me that you made a guest appearance a few weeks ago but not recently, and it also seems that you're slipping a bit with your fine payments and I did hear.... '

Those holes in the door did suggest that there might have been 'issues' and I worried about it for a while. But that was another virtue of the job; there were always plenty of other things to worry about. So he soon slid down my list of risks to be managed and eventually he fell off altogether

Anon

PROBATION MEMORIES OF A FOND NATURE

In the 1980s I worked in a prison. I particularly remember a parole report I did on a young man of Caribbean heritage. I will call him Melvin.

When reading through his file I noticed the casual racism with which previous police, prison and court documents were imbued: assumptions and prejudices thinly disguised as analysis of offending. I worked hard to make sure that what I wrote did not contain assumptions and prejudices like this. I sat down with Melvin when I had finished the report and asked him to read through it and let me know if he was unhappy with anything. The report went in and after his interview with members of the parole board, Melvin was paroled. Of course, you don't say goodbye to a client in these circumstances. You just do your job and then they disappear from your life.

About five years later I was walking through my local park with my dogs and 6-year-old son. A black man with long dreadlocks came jogging towards us. As he approached us he stopped, grabbed me by the arms and kissed me on the cheek. He said 'Thank you Miss.' It was Melvin.

Any probation officer reading this will know that we don't get many a thank you for what we do and can understand how much it meant to me. Probation practice could be tough at times but my overwhelming recollection is that it was a privilege to work with people and try to make a difference in their lives, however small.

The other thing that stands out in my memory is the level of support and professional guidance I always had from colleagues. There was always someone on hand to share a challenging case, talk through possible recommendations or just unburden oneself of the very distressing thing someone might have told you during a PSR interview.

When I later joined a University department where many colleagues were competitive and rivalrous, the absence of this support was very apparent and for me, sorely missed.

Marilyn J. Gregory

A BRICKLAYER'S TALE

I was asked to prepare a report for the Divorce Court, following an application by a serving prisoner who wished to have contact with his son. The man, A, was due for release in 3 months. He was separated from his partner (L), the mother of his son.

I interviewed the mother in the first instance. She related a history of extreme violence by A such that she was fearful of any possible contact with him in the future.

One particular incident that she told me, and I have no reason to disbelieve it, still chills me when I think about it.

L was a prostitute and her pimp was her partner A. He controlled her fiercely. On this occasion L told me that A considered she had committed a misdemeanour that demanded punishment.

Consequently he bound and gagged her, bundled her into a car and drove to a deserted building site in the country. He selected a half built house on the site. He then placed her between two partially built walls and continued the bricklaying work until he had bricked her in entirely. He left her there for four days.

She survived and started a new life in a different part of the country. The court denied contact between him and his son.

Anon

A PRISONER'S PRANK

CK was a well-known offender who had mental health issues and who behaved bizarrely. His background was that he had served in the SAS and was an extremely strong and fit man.

One of the many stories about him is that he was arrested by the local police and placed in a small holding cell at the police station. When the cell was checked, no prisoner could be seen. The cell door was opened and nobody was there. It was impossible that he could have escaped. An actual true locked room mystery!

Then, a snigger was heard from within the cell and on examination CK was found to be spread-eagled across the ceiling, holding his whole body rigid with the strength of his fingers and toes, as a prank to amuse himself, if not the police.

Richard Martin

THOSE 1970s, OR WHEN
THINGS WERE BETTER....

Back in the old days, Probation was so much brilliantly better than it is today, all the old duffers will tell you that. Except that, even though we had that brilliantly better Probation, it didn't stop crime completely – or even very much – did it?

The difference from then to now is that POs were told to get alongside and help clients (advise, assist and befriend) rather than risk assess and manage offenders. The big debate in the 1970s was "Care or Control"?

Most commentators seemed to favour one option whilst recognizing the importance of the other. Whatever side you were on, at least there was a debate. Even then, though, lots of people found reasons to opt out of taking real action about anything, 'I'm not confirmed yet.' 'My senior would have my guts for garters if I signed that petition.' 'I can see both sides of the argument.' 'It's all right for you but I've got a mortgage," etc.

I started as a PO in Newcastle under Lyme on August 1st 1977. I was extremely fortunate to work with John Hague who started a fortnight before me and was a quite outstanding PO. Apart from his caseload

John ran a clients' football team and weekend activities for young men and women and also staged an impromptu drop-in facility. He was also fearless!

John and I attended court most days, We both felt that to give of our best we had to feel comfortable – so obviously we never wore jackets or ties, which we knew to be the demeaning uniform of the downtrodden imposed by the oppressive ruling elite. We did though wear political badges such as CND, Right to Work March etc.

Amazingly, it took seven years before we were finally instructed that we had to dress the part not the prat! Naturally, we took out grievances and had jolly japes asserting our right to free speech, freedom of expression and the like. We did finally agree that we would wear a jacket and a tie (in the conventional manner). I oscillated between a crimson corduroy jacket and what could best be described as a beige plumber's jacket – together with a selection of naff ties. John had a lovely sailing club tie whose motif was a "W" – the initial of the club – above an "anchor".

One time I visited a client at Stafford Prison. I had a badge declaring, "Victory to the PLO," on my jumper. At the gate, I was asked about the initials by someone who clearly knew already. I said, "Well, it's not the Probation Liaison Organisation". Hilarious, I know, but a few days later I had a phone call from a Probation colleague in the prison informing me I was now the subject of a local POA motion. In effect, according to the POA, I was barred from the prison. "Great, another badge," I thought. Sadly, I didn't even need to mount a campaign about that; the governor told them they couldn't bar me and the hoo-ha was no more.

Up to the summer of 1979, when we moved to our big new office, we had two ramshackle offices at 6 and 18 King Street. I worked at number 18 above a finance company which never made enough money to invest in repairs. John was at number 6 with an outside toilet.

In those days we had fewer policies so some staff would occasionally bring their dogs to work. One time, John's sheepdog Heyes had given birth to nine puppies. He didn't want to leave them all at home so they all came to the office, along with Heyes of course – not to mention three other dogs belonging to other officers. Word got round and everybody (and their dog) was coming into the office to see the puppies and obviously the other dog owners proudly displayed their dogs too. We could have written a treatise on canine centred diversion theory, four decades before it became fashionable.

Can anything from those dim and distant days be of importance and indeed relevance for today? All I can do is second the sentiment set out by Howard Davies in Probe 2017: "I'm retired. You're important now. You decide."

Mick Gough

CATS AND DOGS

I was covering court duty as a rookie probation officer in Barnsley in the 1980s when, late one afternoon, we were called back just as the court was adjourning for the day.

Police on the A1 had pulled over a young couple in a hopelessly un-roadworthy car. It then transpired that they were homeless, with all their possessions in the car along with a puppy and a kitten. By the time they had all the facts, the police were bitterly regretting not having let them drive on past.

The situation caused a lot of head scratching in court. The offence would not merit a remand in custody but yet the couple had nowhere to go and no friends or relatives in that part of the country. The car could not be allowed back on the road and they were going to be dealt with the next day in court. In the meantime, arrangements had to be made for the night.

I was asked to find out if they could go to a probation hostel and went off to make enquiries. By this time, a more senior colleague was assisting me and eventually places were found in two different hostels. Then came the bombshell: the police no longer had access to any kennels and the dog and cat had become an issue. We were asked if we could find them accommodation.

I now know that the correct answer to this question was 'no, it's nothing to do with us. We found you the probation hostels. Over and out.'

However, and I'm not sure how this came about, we found ourselves agreeing to each taking one animal home for the night. I took the kitten and my colleague, whose two boys had always wanted a dog, took the puppy.

All went smoothly with the kitten in a cardboard box and I returned it to the office next day. My colleague, however, arrived in looking shattered. All had gone well with the pup until mid-evening when there was a knock at her door, one of the boys answered it and the pup shot straight out of the door and under a car. There followed a chaotic interlude of traumatised children and a late night search for a vet with an out-of- hours service. Then a big bill to pay and an overnight nursing job. I hope I'm right in thinking that the vet's bill was paid from the 'poor box'.

I never had any issue at all about refusing to have anything to do with clients' pets after that.

Hilary Rock

DARE TO BE A DANIEL

After a lifetime working in the Probation Service perhaps the one issue which makes me most angry is the systematic plan to ensure that we are no longer able to exercise our professional judgement.

This had previously been the cornerstone of our training and approach to turning around the lives of the clients placed in our charge by society.

National Standards

For me, the first major step in de-professionalising the Probation Service began with the introduction of National Standards in 1992.

Although dressed up as a well-intentioned system to ensure consistency across the service, some of us recognised from day one that this would reduce our professional discretion and that practitioners would be seriously de-skilled as a result. It was a first step towards fundamentally changing the nature of probation.

We soon saw the first moves to close down opposition, independence of thought and any semblance of professional respect and consultation with practitioners who dared to challenge the new orthodoxy.

I have vivid recall of the Napo AGM which first addressed this issue, and a magnificent speech from Jeremy Cameron of the Action Group which brought the house down.

He precisely predicted what would happen to the Service if we accepted National Standards, said he had no intention of complying with them and urged us all to do the same.

In a memorable phrase he said there might be rare occasions when his files aligned with National Standards, but this would not be because of any conscious action on his part to bring this about. Rather, it was much like the stars and planets in the galaxy - sometimes they too found themselves in alignment but not at the behest of any human intervention (least of all the Home Office).

It so happened that a very senior civil servant who was charged with implementing the standards was observing the debate as a guest to Conference, and he hit the roof!

Jeremy's Chief Probation Officer was immediately instructed to hold a file inspection to check Jeremy's compliance with the standards, and implement disciplinary proceedings when, as suspected, they would fail the test and a very fearless and articulate troublemaker could be swept away.

Hilariously, what actually happened was that the investigation did take place and, as we all anticipated, Jeremy passed with flying colours as the quality of his work was renowned in the area and he easily exceeded the miserable version given for the future of the Service.

Of course later versions of National Standards became more prescriptive, punitive and process driven, and sanctions against staff failing to meet them became more serious, to the extent that few had the strength and clarity of purpose to challenge openly as Jeremy had done.

Nonetheless, many found this lead inspiring, and it made us more resolved to continue to exercise sound professional judgement in dealing with a caseload of real clients with complex and demanding needs.

Enforcement

Enforcement played another key role in ensuring that Community Orders were managed to the virtual exclusion of professional discretion, with a huge rise in prison sentences and disastrous consequences for the lives of many of our clients.

The twin aims of increased punishment and dangling the commercial carrot of making huge profits from Probation coincided beautifully when Curfews came on the scene as a sanction for the first breach of a Community Order.

I'm proud to recall that I never recommended a single Curfew Order during this appalling time in our history.

I always put forward an alternative, using examples from the guidelines to justify my professional recommendation to the Court. It made me extremely unpopular with some managers and sentencers , but I will always maintain that good practice, professional judgement and natural justice should be defended in all circumstances.

The true reason why Curfews were being pushed so hard was to tempt the private companies. I kept asking in meetings how much they were charging the probation service (and ultimately, of course, the taxpayer) in what was laughingly referred to as a 'pilot project'. Eventually the figure inadvertently slipped out and the true potential for huge profits for zero benefit to anyone except the tagging company became clear.

Six nights of tags were costing up to seven times the cost of running an entire Community Order for a year.

Soon after, my line manager called me in to say he'd been instructed to tell me to stop referring to these inconvenient truths. It was to take another ten years or so before it was officially acknowledged that my analysis was correct.

Clients

It's worth recording that the word 'client' was officially banned from the lexicon of probation, as, indeed, the very term 'probation' was to be a few years later.

It was a small but important example of the power of language and the subliminal messages we seek to value, or not, when describing the people with whom we work.

Despite being considered a disciplinary offence to use the term client, I'm proud to say that the obnoxious alternative, 'offender' never passed my lips, and, thanks to the richness of the English language, I was always able to use alternative descriptions, such as calling people by their name.....

One incident is worthy of recording, to illustrate the damage that a de-humanising, de-personalised attitude towards our work can cause.

A very experienced colleague who had previously been a psychiatric social worker took a phone call one morning from a young man he'd been working with for over a year.

He'd rung to tell my colleague that he saw no point in carrying on any longer and planned to commit suicide later that morning. He'd phoned to say goodbye and to tell my colleague not to think this was his fault and to thank him for being so kind and patient with him, but that was his decision.

My colleague encouraged him to come in to the office immediately and after some persuasion he agreed to do so.

As we know, Officers were no longer allowed to have their own offices, so an inadequate number of interview rooms were bookable in short slots throughout the day - never enough to meet demand.

The client duly arrived and my colleague began the complex task of trying to persuade his client to go to hospital, and simultaneously try to secure a bed.

After the normal twenty minute interview slot had elapsed, an office manager instructed that the room must now be vacated as it was needed for the next interview. Despite being told of the sensitive circumstances, nonetheless there was an insistence that the room must be vacated. My colleague was told that if he failed to comply with the instruction he would be reported under the disciplinary code.

Needless to say, my colleague was not deterred from dealing with his client and effectively said he'd be happy to attend a future disciplinary hearing if it was pursued, but please leave him in peace to deal with a life threatening situation.

Fortunately, there was a successful outcome, and of course the threatened disciplinary proceedings never materialized.

Cyril Cleary

FREDDY

Freddy came from what was, in the 1960s, called a problem family: a large family whose numerous members were all known to various social work departments. But it was to probation that the task fell of working with Freddy and his younger brother Alfie.

Both were in their late teens and both were petty criminals. They seldom if ever collected state benefits, unable to cope with the accompanying officialdom. Each instead made a precarious living by keeping and selling rabbits, for human consumption not as pets; by totting, local parlance for collecting and selling scrap metal; and of course by petty thieving. It was this latter activity that brought them into fairly constant contact with the Probation Service. When we were not writing court reports on them we were supervising them on probation, detention centre licence or Borstal after care. They kept us busy.

But it was Freddy, with his wild staring eyes and a shock of disorderly hair, who occupied us most. Alfie seldom kept appointments, preferring to call in on the off chance he might scrounge some cash from our welfare fund. He was also the less delinquent of the two. Freddy on the other hand kept his appointments and more. He frequently called in just to have a chat, sometimes to relate details of his latest adventure or misadventure, sometimes for no apparent purpose. On one occasion he recounted how he had purchased twelve rumbabas, a syrup and sugar soaked cake, and devoured them all at one sitting.

On another occasion he turned up at the office on Xmas Eve and after some desultory chat asked me if I enjoyed rabbit. I said I did, very much. Without a word he ran from the office. He returned ten minutes later breathless and carrying a blood stained, newspaper wrapped parcel. A rabbit freshly killed and skinned minutes before. I think of his action with fondness. He could express his feelings only in actions not words.

Freddy was a troubled soul. While he could not speak of the devils that troubled him they were there, dark and threatening. Probation was, however, good for him. It gave him somewhere to go when things were too much for him. It gave him a refuge, somewhere to be more at ease. Although it possibly did not prevent his offending it did perhaps enable him to delay the fate that seemed inevitably to await him.

And Freddy did offend again and having been previously to Borstal was inevitably sentenced to Borstal recall. I visited him in the Borstal recall institution housed in the old Reading jail, famously known as the prison in which Oscar Wilde had been interned. For young offenders such as Freddy it represented a severe, harsh regime and one which clearly caused him pain, strain and stress. Suffering which showed on his face but of which he still could not speak.

Several weeks later I received a phone call from a Reading Assistant Governor (AG). Could I visit him as soon as possible to discuss Freddy? This I did and was shown into the AG's office. He explained their concern over Freddy's welfare. He had made repeated and genuine attempts at suicide and was a real concern. He explained that in an attempt to curtail Freddy's attempts on his life they had ensured there was nothing in his cell or on his clothing which could be used to harm himself. He had responded by laboriously removing the beading around his mattress, attempting to hang himself with this, having only been prevented by a warden's timely visit.

At this point Freddy himself arrived, having been sent for by the AG. His face wore its usual sheepish grin, an expression which did not alter even when the AG gave him a mighty thwack round the back of the head. Seemingly in the Borstal Recall Unit this passed for a friendly greeting. Freddy's muttered responses to questions put to him by the AG did nothing to explain his suicide attempts and he was soon dismissed from the meeting.

He was, said the Assistant Governor, 'a difficult case.' Could I suggest anything to assist? I stated that I had come to believe that Freddy found being locked up so oppressive that he would seek relief in the most dramatic of ways and so sought release in the only way open to him, suicide. I suggested that to prevent a possible tragic end to this situation he be released back on licence without delay. Rather to my surprise my suggestion was followed and Freddy was released a week or two later.

Freddy finished his licence period without re-offending but later, long after I had moved on, I heard of his ultimate fate. He had been arrested on further theft charges and held overnight in the local police cells. There he had been found the following morning hanging, alone in the cell, having met his final tragic end.

John Dessauer

HOLLOWAY

I'd been working at the prison for a couple of years in the 1990s when I was asked to prepare a parole report on one of the women in the psychiatric unit, C1, which I was covering.

GC was several years into quite a long sentence for arson with intent, having set fire to a building she lived in which was also home to other people. We met a couple of times and it was clear to me that I would be unable to support release on parole at that stage. She had mental health issues and future behaviour was hard to predict.

When I had finished the report, I went to the unit to go through it with GC. I briefly explained to the unit officer that I was not recommending parole and they called her to the office and said they would find us a room.

We walked down the corridor and round a few bends to a part of the unit which was well out of sight or earshot of the prison officers' rooms. There was of course no CCTV in those days. A door was opened and we were ushered into a room. I had a split second to register that it would be wise to tell the officer that this was not a suitable room, and another split second to think what an insult it would be to declare in front of this vulnerable young woman that I did not feel safe being left there alone with her. I opted to keep quiet and talk as tactfully and respectfully as possible, focusing on how she could work towards a more favourable response next parole review. I breathed a huge sigh of relief when I left the unit still in one piece.

Within a couple of days, the Discipline report on GC landed on my desk, late as always (sometimes they didn't come at all). As I opened the printout it was almost as tall as me and was a complete catalogue of violent acts against prison staff and inmates.

A short time later, I was walking down the corridor on the unit when I saw GC about to pass an ageing Principal Officer who barked some short rebuke at

her. Within seconds, the PO had hit the ground hard and GC was laying into her.

Bells rang and officers appeared from all directions. It took several of them to get the situation under control and be able to cart GC off.

I think I was lucky to have got away with my reckless decision.

Hilary Rock

(Mis)MANAGEMENT

The steady degradation of public services reached its ideological zenith in the 1980s, the heyday of Thatcherism whose destructive legacy and lasting damage to our social fabric still resonate.

Remember managerialism? It was highly fashionable then and before long it turned its malevolent gaze on the Probation Service. At the office where I worked it coincided unhappily with the arrival of a new chief officer. Many who rise through the ranks to senior positions in public service lack the aptitude or ability. He was no exception.

At our first meeting I recall his obvious desire to make an impact and to introduce 'accountability' into the service. It was obviously difficult to argue with this but we soon learned that it meant far more centralised control and direction. It also coincided with the new, dominant, down to earth, common sense 'what works' and its more sophisticated but equally vague associate 'evidence based practice'. Leaving aside who was to determine what worked or what constituted evidence, the future focus on managing 'offending behaviour' was to change fundamentally the way the service operated.

An early casualty was the service's presence in the courts, where we had zealously cultivated an influential role as an 'officer of the court'. Indeed until one of the many reorganisations we were managed at county level by a group of magistrates reflecting the service's origins as police court missionaries.

Reducing our representation in the courts to one of a mere administrative presence, and rarely by an actual PO, completely undermined our role which had rested on a belief that justice was better served by our presence. We were often consulted, enabling sentencing decisions to be better informed and to be seen to be so. However, the relationship which many of us had developed with magistrates and judges sat uneasily with the new model of tighter central control and so, unsurprisingly, it slowly disappeared.

So too did 'Aftercare' from our title. Before long prison visits, which had been an essential part of helping to prepare prisoners for release, were a thing of the past.

It was during these times of rapid upheaval that I left the service. Twelve years had worn me out and I think I really did see the writing on the wall heralding a service which I no longer recognised and which betrayed the origins and ethos of the work. What was happening was a complete departure from the social work model to one driven by policing and enforcement. This required a different approach to comply with 'what works'.

The social work model was holistic and encompassed all aspects of a client's life - social interactions, education, employment, housing, relationships etc. - all that makes people what they are. We saw offending behaviour as a part of the whole picture and that it is best addressed by working with the client on all these levels; this enabled them to review their offending and develop alternative ways of managing their lives.

While that may sound, and sometimes was, overly optimistic, it did have a coherent philosophy and in many cases offered a real chance of success both in reducing offending and in restoring a sense of dignity and self-worth. This is patently never the case with imprisonment which has been since used on an ever increasing scale.

I recall that in 1975 the then Home Secretary, Roy Jenkins , observing that the prison population was around 43,000, pledged that if it reached 45,000 he would resign. When I looked at the government website today I read 'The prison population was 83,165 as of Friday 17th August 2018.' So something has gone wrong, hasn't it?

I don't think I could have coped with the changes and subsequent demands and I have great respect for my many former colleagues who stuck with it. They were still able to deliver an effective service though at considerable personal cost. Subsequent governments have pretty much wrecked the Service. What a terrible price to pay for political expediency.

Terry Allen

IN THE WAITING ROOM.

It was a quiet afternoon in the probation office. May, the office receptionist, was busying herself doing some filing when a young man staggered into the waiting room and up to the reception hatch. May laid aside her filing.

'What can I do for you, young man?' she queried.

The young man in a strangled voice said, 'I need to see Mrs.W, my probation officer'.

May checked the office diary. 'She's not in, do you want to leave a message?'

The young man, now looking desperate said 'But I've been stabbed!'

Now, May was a very experienced receptionist and knew a thing or two, so had no hesitation in responding. 'Now lad, don't lark about', she said.

May was not, however, prepared for the next event. With a groan the young man slid down the reception hatch ending prone on the floor. May peered through the hatch and was horrified to see blood seeping from his back. She shouted, 'Someone's been stabbed! Call an ambulance!' This brought the staff running only to retreat in confusion when they saw the figure, bleeding and recumbent on the floor.

At this stage a PO, Joan, chanced upon the scene. She took immediate action, pressing a tea towel on to the wound to stem the bleeding while talking to the young man to ensure he did not lose consciousness. In the meantime, 999 calls had summoned both ambulance and police and within minutes sirens and flashing blue lights announced their arrival, police cars and vans screeching to a halt on the paved entrance to the office.

Police officers then scoured the area in search of the assailant. In the meantime the ambulance men had taken over from Joan while commending her for her speedy actions which they said had prevented further bleeding. The young man continued to look both shocked and terrified. He clearly thought he was about to die. As he was stretchered to the ambulance, the scene, police cars, ambulance, flashing blue lights and hurrying police officers resembled a scene from the Bronx.

Later, the events leading to the incident became clear. The young man, the victim, was a sixth former at a nearby school. He had been walking to the probation office when another pupil began exchanging words, ending with him being stabbed.

Fortunately the wound proved not as serious as initially thought and he made a full recovery. Did the case ever come to court? I think not, my memory telling me that the young man declined to identify his assailant. Just another day in the probation office.

Marie Clarke

DUMB FRIENDS – NOT SO DUMB

And of course, the Probation Service never used to be entirely about crime….

Some of us worked in Divorce Court Welfare, working with families in dispute about the arrangements for the children. Some situations were truly awful, with sexual and/or physical abuse within the family. But most parents that came to us from the Divorce Court were good parents, who loved their children but were hurt or angry with the other parent.

A good while ago, we were allowed to bring our dogs to work. Mine (Tessa) was a placid and friendly

Golden Retriever who would be asleep by the radiator most of the time. Golden Retrievers (amongst other dogs) can pick up on people's emotions and one particular occasion stays with me.

I was interviewing the children's mother, who was very upset and became tearful. Obviously it was inappropriate to do what you'd do with a friend and give a hug. I watched as Tessa got up and walked slowly over to her, stood looking at her with those big brown Retriever eyes and put her head in this lady's lap, looking up at her and gently wagging her tail.

Well, that was just what this lady needed, a massive release of emotions, crying and hugging the dog.

Anyway, matters were eventually resolved by agreement and we never heard any more. Until I got a call from reception to say Mrs xxx was here and could she have a word please. It was rather nice to learn that everything was going smoothly with the children and could she please give these doggy treats for Tessa.

There's another divorce tale, about a father who, unusually, gained custody of their baby daughter – the right decision. I got a call from reception saying Mr xxx would like to ask for some advice. He wanted to discuss some concerns he had about his 15 year old daughter. For the life of me I couldn't place him and asked a few questions – how long ago did this take place? – Where did he live at the time? It transpired I'd written a report for the Court some 15 years earlier when his child was a baby and he kept the Welfare

Report in his bedside table, looking at it to reassure himself at times of self-doubt. We'd moved offices three times since the report was written… no mean feat to track us down after 15 years!

David Butterworth

STRIKE!!!

The first ever strike in the Probation Service took place in North East London in 1982.

London was then divided into five areas, or in some cases fiefdoms. The particular fief, in N.E. London, had at its helm Don Moore. He had his good points, let's just say that.

Don Moore wanted to sack a very popular senior and he employed a hatchet man, whom we will call 007, to do it. The senior was sacked and the branch debated a motion of no confidence in the CPO and a proposal for a one day strike.

The quorum for a branch meeting was something like eighteen. The hall that day had over eighty people in it.

I had just arrived in the area and knew none of the people involved. The motion was proposed by a fiery young Welsh speaking woman. (She proposed the motion in English.) It was seconded by an East End communist ex-bricklayer, the late great Terry Bowers. 'Hello', I thought, 'someone's got organised here'. It was the Action Group.

In those days almost all the workforce had grown up in the sixties and seventies, but some before. Some had been battle hardened by action elsewhere; most were politicised one way or another by national turmoil. After the optimism and hope of the sixties, Thatcher was in power.

In the hall debate raged. 'I can't abandon my clients,' said someone. She was asked how they managed at weekends. Questions were asked about tactics, publicity, whether it was right to strike. Surprising alliances were formed or broken. Joan Findlay chaired this roller coaster with tact and skill, aided by Sally Morris as secretary. It came to the vote. (Incidentally Terry Bowers once made a speech at NAPO AGM in which he proclaimed, 'When you see that lot on the telly' – he named names – 'doncha just want to give them a damn good kicking?' He was monitored. He also once took out a grievance against Don Moore for directing him to move office. No one knew what to do with a grievance, so it consisted of Bowers and Moore sitting in an office together, 'I ain't fuckin' going,' said Terry. 'You are fuckin' going,' said Don Moore. And Moore was right.)

There were several resolutions in the vote and the proposers had made the mistake of lumping all the resolutions together to be voted on; so, if you disagreed with one, you in effect voted against all four. The vote was lost.

Joan agreed to put them again, this time separately. The vote to strike was won.

It was momentous. All the people who had voted against the motion respected the outcome. Well, almost all. The picket lines were a massive success, well organised by the strike committee. A mass meeting was held afterwards with speakers from NAPO head office. It was a day of heartening solidarity, integrity and humour which politicised the work force and probably the whole of NAPO.

My part in it was, since I knew nothing about it, to make the sandwiches. Because this was a strike I thought the proletarian workers would want jam sandwiches. I made a mountain of them. They were not popular. Where were the vol au vents? (Vol au vents were popular in 1982.)

The effects of the strike were remarkable. The Home Office came down, staff were listened to and systems were set up. The chief was a changed man.

A few years later, the hatchet man appeared in my office and asked me to represent him in his own battles with the chief. Then and thereafter he always said that sacking the senior was the worst mistake of his life.

Jeremy Cameron

NORMAL FOR BESWICK

At Beswick we had a well known female drunk whom we regularly let sleep it off on an empty office floor.

Unfortunately she turned up one evening when the staff Christmas party was in full swing (in the days when alcohol was allowed on the premises) and for obvious reasons it was deemed unwise to let her in.

So the two SPOs decided to try and coax her into the Mini owned by one of them and give her a lift home instead.

Both SPOs had glasses and beards.

As she was being pushed into the car, our client looked up and said:

'I'm not getting into a car with a probation officer with two fucking heads!'

Gill Scott

G

I was ordered by a judge to prepare a report to consider contact by a serving prisoner with his two young sons. He had a history of violence. He was due for release having served an eight-year sentence for attempting to murder his wife, the mother of his sons.

During interviews with G in prison, and gathering further information, it became clear that G was not so much interested in having contact with his sons as in finishing his violence towards his wife.

The Judge considered my report, and other information, and decided to deny contact; and also to agree that the police should move G's wife and the children to a different part of the country for their safety. G was given this information prior to his release from his sentence.

G then wrote to me and to the police who had been actively involved in his case, stating that he would deal with us when he was released from prison. The police took this threat seriously, and decided to follow G on his release to see that he did not carry out any threats. At the same time they came to see my wife and me at our home. They advised us of means of escaping from our house should G break in and take us hostage or try to harm us. (The police considered that G would think that I would be able to give him information to lead him to his wife and family.) The Probation Service paid for my house to be made more secure.

The police followed G and reported to me on a regular basis. G had found another woman friend and had settled. After 12 months, however, G discovered that his new partner was having a relationship with another man. G murdered the other man. He then tried to hang himself in local woods. He failed.

G was arrested and remanded in custody at the local prison, where within seven days he died, having hanged himself in his cell.

Anon

NOT THE BRIGHTEST

THE CASE OF THE BUNGLED BURGLARY....

Many years ago, one of the men on the books of the Probation Service decided that easy access could be had to the jewellery shop on the ground floor of the Probation Office.

In due course, after no doubt considerable planning and "casing the joint"and whilst reporting to his probation officer, he broke into the probation office one night, went to the floor immediately over the jewellery shop and gained entry to the shop by taking up a couple of floor boards, knocking a hole in the ceiling of the jeweller's and dropping himself into the shop. He then selected what he fancied and went to leave.

Unfortunately for him, but fortunately for everyone else, the shop had rather better locks than the probation office and he couldn't break out. Neither could he climb back through the hole in the ceiling…nothing to stand on and the hole was too high to reach.

Next morning, when the shopkeeper arrived, our burglar was found fast asleep in an armchair with his bag filled to the brim…..

WAR OF INDEPENDENCE

The Film "Revolution" (1985) starred Al Pacino, Donald Sutherland, Nastassja Kinski, Joan Plowright and a number of "Extras" from King's Lynn. One of the Extras, well known to the local Police and Probation Service and several other agencies in town, decided during a gap in filming to nip along to sign on for his benefit. Needless to say, arriving to sign on wearing the uniform of a seventeenth century soldier was not his most sensible move that day….

ROBBERY ATTEMPT AT THE POST OFFICE:

And then there was the wonderfully inept attempted robbery of the Post Office. Two men, in a car, cruising slowly and repeatedly past the post office, were noticed by the police as, I think the expression is, 'acting suspiciously'. In due course, they ran out of the post office and were pursued by police. They did their best to escape on foot, but running away in a town you don't know well is not likely to be successful when you run down a street blocked by a tall brick wall at the end!

(One of the two was the same man that broke into the jewellery shop above.)

David Butterworth

SENTIMENTAL NOSTALGIC STORY

One day I got a call from reception. John S**** would like to speak to you. I hadn't seen or heard from John for years, but remembered him well, so was happy to take the call.

It had occurred to him out of the blue to let me know how he was getting on. He was doing well, in the second year of a degree course, working part time to support himself and feeling good about life.

Three years earlier he had been on Parole and was struggling to get away from a life style that had done him no good for a long time. He had turned up at the office, on a day he didn't have an appointment and was desperate to see me.

The previous day he had been on a bender. He had woken up on a bed in an unfamiliar room. Also in the bed was a woman. He had no idea who she was. Between them lay a shotgun. For a minute he didn't know if she was alive or dead. She was alive, but in those first waking moments, John had a 'road to Damascus' revelation, which had brought him straight to my office, pausing only to throw the shotgun in the river. (Our reception staff were pretty resilient but people arriving with firearms could spook them.)

During a long career in the Probation Service, you hear a lot of statements of intent from people, to the effect that they have changed, will never offend again etc. etc. Sometimes it is said because they think this is what the probation officer wants to hear, on a lot of occasions I'm sure they mean it at the time. However, it doesn't always pan out as both sides would have wanted.

Sometimes though you see someone who has truly reached a crossroads, and that morning it was not rocket science to realise that John had not only meant it, but was wholly committed to doing what was necessary to achieve it. This was a one-time opportunity not to be missed. He knew he had to get away from his current lifestyle and connections.

I spent the next few hours trawling hostels and sweet talking other Probation areas to take the case. By the end of the day he was on a coach to a town hundreds of miles away, where he did, it appears, turn his life around.

I wonder if the Probation services we have today would have the flexibility I was able to tap into then? Probably not. But now or then, a phone call like the one I had that day makes the job feel worthwhile for a long time.

Anne King

MORE 1980s

Whilst I was living in Stoke and working at the Newcastle under Lyme office in the 1980s, I had a client whom I shall call Peter.

Peter had been a safe cracker (hence my name for him) and I took him on as a new parolee. He had just completed 4 years of a much longer sentence, most of which he had spent in HMP Dartmoor.

Peter and I developed a good relationship and he worked hard at rebuilding his life with his wife whom I'll call Meg. She had faithfully visited him every week during his sentence – not that easy a journey from a village outside Stoke. Meg had a poorly paid but regular job but Peter didn't find it easy to get employment.

Work was hard to come by at that time. The steelworks, where he used to work, had closed down, the potteries were in recession as there hadn't been a royal birth or marriage for some time and the mines were in upheaval as a result of the strike.

Peter kept all his appointments with me and he kept going for job interview after job interview. He was always upfront with potential employers and stressed his determination to build a new life for himself and

Meg, but many could not see past the image of "serious criminal" that Dartmoor Prison conjured up.

As so often is the case the banana skin that led to him slipping up had been left in front of him by the Department of Health and Social Security – a double misnomer of a department. Meg, who by now was heavily pregnant, was having quite a lot of time off work and money was very tight. One Friday night in desperation as they had no money for food, Peter stole some cigarettes from the local post office which he then sold.

The police described the break in as very professional in that the windows had been drilled and the alarms bypassed. It wasn't long before his name came up. Peter admitted what he had done. He was mortified he had let Meg down just when she was going to need his support the most. He was remanded in custody.

Unbeknown to Peter I had just that day managed to find an employer who was prepared to give him a job. The employer hesitated a bit when I told him what had happened but stuck with his offer of employment.

Unfortunately, Hanley Crown Court was not so forgiving and they sentenced Peter to three years in prison. I stood firmly behind my recommendation of a probation order and Peter's barrister and solicitor encouraged him to appeal.

Three months later Peter's appeal was due to be heard at the Court of Appeal.

I travelled down to London with my wife Anna. Neither of us had ever been to the Court of Appeal so it was a new experience. (When we saw all the costumed court personnel and all the solicitors in their Savile Row suits Anna was worried that I was a bit too casually dressed. She thought my off white cotton jacket made me look like the milkman.)

I found my way to the probation office where I met a very angry senior probation officer who demanded to know why, as an officer of the court, I hadn't followed established etiquette and informed him of my intention to attend. I apologized, saying that I had never heard of such a requirement, but I was there to support my client and the recommendation I had made in my report. This only seemed to enrage him further, particularly as I wasn't wearing a suit.

'Don't you know where you are?' he demanded. 'This is the Court of Appeal. You don't recommend Probation at the Court of Appeal. You will have to amend it!'

I asked him to show me where this was stipulated in the Court Etiquette rules he had referred to. I declined to amend the report, wondered whether he had forgotten the word Probation in Senior Probation Officer and took my leave.

I found Peter's solicitor who introduced me to the QC who was representing him. The appeal was being heard by Lord Lane (then the Lord Chief Justice) and Lord Salisbury. I asked the barrister to consider calling me to give evidence so that I could back up my recommendation in person. I also showed him a report from the prison probation officer to the Parole Board that supported my report. He asked me whether he could submit it but I declined as it wasn't mine to give him. 'However,' I said, 'if Lord Lane would like to see it who am I to refuse him?'

We were called into court. It was a large room with bookcases, presumably full of ancient law books, on each side. Their Lordships were due to be seated on a high raised platform. The only person at a similar level was the person in the dock: Peter.

We were told to 'All rise' and the two Law Lords in their more resplendent robes and wigs entered. Just after we sat down there was a bit of a commotion as a very frail, elderly man in a rather tatty wig and gown entered and bowed. He proceeded to push a long ladder slowly along the left hand book shelves. The court went very quiet as he gingerly mounted the ladder and climbed up. No one was sure whether he would make it. He found the book he wanted and climbed gingerly down, and everyone breathed a sigh of relief. It was a surreal moment. I had expected Lord Lane to say, 'Carruthers, you haven't paid the fine on the last book you took out,' but nothing was said and he slowly left the court.

The hearing resumed and Peter's barrister told the court that I was present and that he would like to call me. Lord Lane said he would like to hear from me so I mounted the steps to the high dais where I was sworn in. (I affirmed.) After a few preliminary questions to verify I was the author of the Social Enquiry Report and to check that I stood by my recommendation, Peter's barrister asked me whether I also had a report about Peter that had been written by the prison probation officer for the Parole Board. I said, 'Yes' and Lord Lane said, 'I would like to read that'. I handed it over, job done!

This report supported mine and the author identified that Peter seemed committed to working with the support that probation could provide to turn his life around and build a home with Meg and their child.

Lord Lane then turned to me and took his wig off. (Lord Salisbury followed suit.) 'Let's have a more informal chat,' he said. The two of them then got me to talk and answer some searching questions about the nature of our relationship and his relationship with Meg. Lord Lane wanted to know why I felt it was worth taking a risk with Peter.

After what felt like hours but may have been only about ten minutes, the two Lords turned to confer between themselves. Then Lord Lane turned back to me and said, 'I don't think I can go as far as a Probation Order. Would you be happy with a Suspended Sentence Supervision Order?' 'That would be fine by me,' I replied. 'Good,' he said. 'Can you give him a lift home?'

Peter was in tears as we left. We called in at the probation office, just in case there were any more Court Etiquette requirements to comply with before we left. The Senior Probation Officer wasn't free to talk with me unfortunately.

Peter completed the order without any further mishaps.

John Hague

STRANGE HAPPENINGS

I was working as a probation officer in a small town at the top of the Welsh valleys. I worked from an office above the old court room. It was a sunny afternoon and I had just had my lunch in the local authority canteen situated at the other side of the town square.

I was feeling a little sluggish. I had a list of afternoon appointments to interview people for court reports. The first client of the afternoon had committed an offence of GBH and had a long string of previous convictions.

I climbed the rickety old stairs back up to the probation office. The first client was on time and waiting for me, sitting on a chair on the landing which served as a waiting room. I called him into my office. He was tall, slim, in his mid 20s, wearing jeans - nothing out of the ordinary.

Yet immediately there was a frisson in the air. I employed a little 'reflection-in-action' to work out what was happening but I couldn't quite put my finger on it. My heart was beating rapidly: I had never experienced this type of reaction to a stranger before.

I kept my composure and carried on with the interview. Whilst we were talking I noticed he had amateurishly tattooed LOVE across the fingers of his right hand and HATE across the fingers of his left. Still my heart was beating fast.

We discussed the offence which involved him having head butted another man in a local public house. When I enquired about his motivation for the offence, he simply explained that the other man had put his face too close to his. He said that his actions were not unreasonable as anyone would respond in the same way and suggested that I might too, given a similar situation. This was somewhat surprising and I told him this was not a good excuse, that it would not be my natural reaction, nor would it be usual behaviour for many people.

We discussed my recommendation for community service. The interview was coming to a close and despite talking about quite abhorrent behaviour and the great divide between us, I still felt an electricity in the room. As he stood up to leave, he grabbed my hand with his right hand (the fingers tattooed with LOVE) and said rather wistfully 'If only we had met under different circumstances'. Then he left.

I could hardly breathe.

I never saw him again: I don't remember how he was sentenced. I was a Probation Officer for 16 years and never had that reaction to anyone else, hence it still being vividly imprinted on my memory.

Anon

OFF TO MARBA

While interviewing my young female (rather strident) client who was on licence, all was going well until she informed me she was off on holiday to 'Marba for a few weeks with me mates', and 'wouldn't be in for a bit'.

I reminded her that she was on licence and if there was any chance of her going away for a few weeks – let alone out of the country - then she would have to bring in flight tickets and the address of where she was going and I would copy it and request permission on her behalf which would take a while. But she insisted that she was 'goin' next week!'

She was now getting really angry and refused downright to bring in any proof of where or when she was going so I said that without a copy of tickets or address it was out of the question. Taking another tack, she asked what would happen if she decided to go and live there. Again I explained she was on licence and was not allowed out of the country except for exceptional circumstances.

This argument went round and round for about ten minutes and was getting pretty heated by this time – so I said I thought it was a good idea to terminate the interview for a bit to cool down. She wasn't having any of it and said she was going away and that was that.

I lost it and said she wasn't f...... going anywhere!

After my very unprofessional outburst she took the high ground and said 'Jackie, I never thought you would use that language!'

I stood chastened and apologized for my lack of decorum and as we were by now entering the waiting room – I asked her to give it ten minutes and we would start again but she pushed her way behind me into the general office still shouting at me. Staff were needed to 'show her the way out'.

I was completely floored and went to see my senior and apologised to him for my bad language, saying that I had become completely exasperated and let the Probation Service down.

To which he replied 'Don't worry Jackie, I hit someone once!'

Jackie Foot

THE COURTEOUS CLERK

Sitting in court day after day one gets to see many characters. Best of all I remember Reginald, the courteous clerk. This was Reginald, the chief clerk, who was a delightful, if old fashioned gentleman. His main interest in life was the study of English literature of the eighteenth and nineteenth century and it may be true to say that his knowledge of such literature surpassed his knowledge of the law. Always polite and fair to all who appeared before the court he was a delight to deal with. However, his lack of worldliness did on occasions lead to events as entertaining as they were bizarre.

On one memorable day he had before him a rather belligerent gent, who was more than a little annoyed at being brought before the court over his failure to pay a past fine. Reginald rose to face the man in the dock to establish first, for the record, his identity.

'What sir, is your name?' enquired Reginald.

The defendant, thinking perhaps of the moon landings that were in the news at the time, replied, 'Apollo'.

Reginald was not at all put out. 'And your first name, Mr. Apollo?' he enquired.

The defendant was ready with his reply. 'Mr. Fucking Apollo,' was his response.

Reginald noted the names for the record then once more addressed the man in the dock. 'Mr. Fucking Apollo, you have yet to pay…..' The details of the non-paid fine continued but by this stage who was listening?

On another occasion, Reginald was required to read a lengthy document, pertinent to the case in hand. Seated at the clerk's desk Reginald's dulcet tones rang around the court. Then, disaster. Reginald's chair collapsed under him, reduced to matchwood. Reginald himself was flung under his desk, disappearing entirely from sight. The court was reduced to a shocked silence.

Then, from beneath the desk came Reginald's voice, picking up from where he had left off as he gradually rose, like a Savile Row suited Neptune rising from the deep. And not perturbed in the least.

An old gent, one of the regulars in the public gallery, began to shout encouragement but was quickly hushed by an usher. A pity really. Reginald's performance was more than deserving of a round of applause, if not an encore.

Marie Clarke

HAZARDS OF DIVORCE COURT
WELFARE WORK

Before the days of enhanced security and planning procedures to adopt in case of emergency, we sort of bumbled along, not expecting any great difficulty we couldn't manage.

However....on this occasion I was interviewing a father who wanted to know where his ex-wife lived. Not a good idea in the circumstances. He was well known in both Divorce and the Criminal Courts and could be violent. His request was politely declined, whereupon he decided to ask for the keys to my filing cabinet. Again, requested declined. At which point he decided to try and persuade me by coming behind me and putting his arm round my neck.

At this time in the Probation Service, there were no alarms of any kind, just the telephone and someone in reception to answer. Despite several attempts to attract attention, all that happened was that I was constantly connected to an outside line, until eventually someone realised that me flashing a light in the general office might indicate a problem. I was able to say 'call the police, "X" has got me round the neck.' Moments later, five police officers plus a dog handler led him away peacefully.

That incident resulted in the issue of personal alarms. I continued as his officer, once being mistaken for his psychiatrist when going to see him in hospital following a car crash. We remained on good terms up to the time of his death.

David Butterworth

WHO KNOWS

On the morning following an away day my SPO said she would like a word with me in her room. I went there to see her. She asked me how I found the previous day's event. I replied that it was a good day team building and I had a good time.

The SPO surprised me saying it was reported to her that I had had a bad day. Moreover, this was reported to her by other managers who had reported this to the ACO who had then asked the SPO to have a word with me about it.

I pointed out that someone must have made a mistake as I clearly enjoyed the content of the day.

The SPO then stated that when she first came to work at our office she thought I was another black probation officer with a similar name whom she described as being, "an angry black man".

I said I found her statement offensive given that the angry black man syndrome was a derogatory label used in the USA when pouring derision on prominent black men. Furthermore, it was debasing that a black female SPO was using this label to describe me and another black male probation officer.

The SPO began to back pedal saying that she did not know me and was basically trying to see if I had any issues, as she had been asked to establish this.

At that very moment the ACO was seen parking in the car park. I told the SPO that I would be taking it up with the ACO. On approaching the ACO I made it clear that I enjoyed the previous day's event but for some unknown reason I was being told that I was observed having a bad day.

The ACO said it was a bit confusing given our own contact on the previous day and added that it was possible the persons observing me and making the report just did not know me.

I explained to the ACO that my journey through life, including the Probation Service has forever consisted of people who do not know me assuming that they do.

Anon

THE OLD MAN AND THE JUDGE

" Your cheese roll is offensive! "

One of the joys of being a probation officer, for me at least, was the time spent in court. Drama, tragedy, comedy, every aspect of life, it was all there.

And the unexpected, that too, always there, waiting for you...

The tedium of a Crown Court hearing in which even the two defendants seemed to have lost interest was suddenly enlivened by an unexpected and excited outburst from the judge.

'That man at the back! Bring him forward. Put him in the dock.'

An old man came forward from the public benches and hesitantly entered the dock to the urging of the court usher. The two defendants looked alarmed and shuffled to the far end of the dock as though fearing a contaminating influence.

The old man looked anxious and clutched the rail of the dock. What had he done? I asked the usher. 'He was eating a cheese roll,' she hissed 'and drinking 7 Up from a can.'

'Search him Mister Dock Officer and find out his name,' ordered the judge.

Accompanied by the prison officer, the old man left the dock to be searched in the cell corridor. The trial continued but our thoughts were elsewhere. What was going to happen? The answer was soon in coming when the old man was returned to the dock by the prison officer.

Once more the trial was stopped. The prison officer gave the old man's name and relieved our anxieties by revealing that the search had been fruitless. No concealed weapons, no drugs, nothing.

Then began the judicial examination.

Judge: 'What were you doing at the back of the court?'

Old man: 'Nothing.'

Judge (accusingly): 'You were eating.'

Old man: 'Oh, that.'

Judge: 'Why were you eating?'

Old man (a little defiantly): 'I was hungry.'

Judge (angrily): 'That's no excuse. You know you are not allowed to eat in court. This is a serious matter.'

Old man: 'Oh, I see.'

Judge (dismissively): 'Oh take him away. Bring him back at two o'clock.'

It was then noon.

The old man, guided by the prison officer, exited to the cells and the trial continued. At two o'clock, after the luncheon adjournment, the old man was produced but waved away back to the cells by the judge. Again at 2.15, then at 2.30. Finally at 2.40 the judge condescended to halt the trial and deal with what had now become the real business of the day - the old man and his transgression.

But never fear, the old man's interests were being looked after. A barrister at a loose end had been rescued from his lonely vigil pacing the court corridors and was to represent the old man.

He rose to his feet, straightened his wig and began to mitigate on behalf of his unexpected client. His mitigation went as follows. The old man was a person of impeccable character who had, until today, never entered a court for any reason. He lived nearby and had worked for a local council all his life until his recent retirement. Now, with nothing to do and time on his hands, he had thought he would go to the court and see British justice in action. Sadly, the barrister concluded, the old man had assumed that the court was like a 'picture house' or a 'football arena' - a place to which you took your packed lunch to consume as the fancy took you. He now understood that courts were not like that and was deeply sorry for his unwitting transgression.

The judge was duly mollified. 'I accept that no contempt was intended,' he pronounced. 'You may leave the dock.'

Without a word the old man left the dock, he left the courtroom, he left the courthouse - all with the greatest rapidity. I suspect he wished he could leave the country.

We who remained in the court-room were left to ponder what the whole episode had been about. Would the image and majesty of the law have been damaged had the old man simply been asked not to eat in court? Had what transpired contained the elements of compassion, humanity and dignity which go in part to make up justice?

We could have asked the old man for his opinion - but he had long gone.

John Dessauer

STRIKE 2

Would you approach the entrance to ACAS with foreboding, curiosity or just plain apprehension?

In 1985 branch representatives of N.E. London NAPO - Chair, Secretary, member and a national officer - asked themselves: what the hell are we doing here?

In 1985 the prison population was 45,000 and the Service was managed on a nationwide/area basis with a Chief, a couple of assistants and a Probation Committee as employer made up of the great and the good but mainly magistrates. In short it was 'localism' with all the advantages of scale and community identification. And all their problems.

An understanding of racial discrimination was central. After the Brixton riots and disturbances of 1981 the Scarman report introduced the concept of institutional racism; but this did little to stem the tide of racist attacks and killings, let alone racial discrimination in the workplace and elsewhere.

The traditional hamlets of Forest Gate and East Ham became the home of many Asian and Black migrants in the 1960s and 1970s. In the 1980s a number of killings of young Asian men took place there. The involvement of the National Front in fomenting these and other attacks was well documented but denied by local councillors, the police and the courts. Pressure groups were formed, among them the Newham Youth Movement and the Newham Monitoring Project. Marches and protests outside Forest Gate police station attracting huge crowds became commonplace.

Meanwhile the Probation Chief and Committee seemed unable to understand that they were on the periphery of a momentous social change where equity in justice was being tested.

Against this background the Forest Gate Probation Office opened in 1983 in a disused factory in a back street of terraced houses, at the centre of the Asian and Black communities. It was an opportunity for an imaginative restructure of previously inadequate provision in Newham. The function was 'to develop and improve services for racial minority offenders'.

Already a drop in centre had been established, attended every day by young black clients seeking advice, attention and sometimes refuge. Now an Asian Woman's Project was created for those experiencing racism in the wider community and often struggling in their own community. The two probation officers in the group had regular consultation with the community. Meanwhile the Homeless Young People's Project was established to provide refuge and accommodation for an epidemic of young black males, many thrown out of home because of their offending. The SPO once labelled 'North East London's golliwog' by the chair of the Probation Committee found himself meeting the sophisticated and understanding Home Secretary, William Whitelaw.

The trial of the Newham Seven began in May 1985. Seven Asian youths and three white youths were charged with Affray. Three of the Asian youths were acquitted, the remainder remanded for SERs (PSRs). The Forest Gate team prepared the reports against a background of duress. The judge, however, praised the reports for their objectivity and professionalism. Community Service Orders resulted.

Then the Chief announced that the Forest Gate office was to close.

The given reason was that staff would merge in a new purpose built office in the centre of the borough. Representations were to no avail. The Chief could not comprehend that uprooting a team that had developed a particular relationship with a minority community would not only broadcast a negative message but would undo all of the enterprise and innovation at a stroke. He was not persuaded that Probation should find new ways to engage with racial minorities.

The branch endorsed a motion to establish a formal dispute. The Probation Committee heard the dispute and asked both sides to try harder to reach agreement. Statistics were exchanged and the fundamental issues were obscured. The Committee sent the matter up the road to the national Joint Negotiating Committee. A meeting was convened at the National Farmers' Union.

On arrival the Chief approached the branch to share what he thought was an amusing account of his journey that day with a magistrate he particularly disliked. In the rigours of London travel a brawl had developed and the hapless JP had been decked.

The JNC was more used to dealing with wage structures and codes and conditions of employment than these issues and they were clearly bemused. The Research and Information officer, a member of the management team, took issue with the Chief about the statistics submitted by the employers. Lunch was not a good advertisement for the agricultural industry; the Chief stood up and said 'Well, you wouldn't come here for the food.' The meeting dragged on and it became clear that the JNC was neither willing to close Forest Gate nor to rule against a Chief. The parties were sent away to try harder once again!

The next twenty one days saw the sides entrenched. Then the next meeting between branch and the Chief and Committee's Secretary was extraordinary.

The branch was told that the process of consultation had ended and the Forest Gate office would be closed in four weeks.

In response the branch chair said: "If that is the case I will go from here immediately to the High Court and apply for an injunction".

Frozen silence. Everyone looked around the room, perhaps seeking an escape route. Then the Committee Secretary, with her hand on the Chief's arm, suggested a short break.

On being asked later about his unplanned intervention the chair simply said he had blurted out the threat in the absence of anything else filling his head and moreover he did not know where the High Court sat or how to serve an injunction.

After the break the branch was informed that, following contact with ACAS, the dispute would move to another stage and another place.

At ACAS the sides were placed in separate rooms. A national NAPO officer represented the branch and with the Conciliator travelled between rooms, first to establish the differences and then with proposals for resolution. The branch was told that never in the history of ACAS had a matter of principle alone been brought for their attention.

By the end of the morning ACAS told both sides that they should go away and try harder (again).

Not much trying took place by either side in the following three weeks and the Chief finally set another closure date.

The branch in response convened an Extraordinary Meeting and the inevitable motion for a one day protest strike was passed unanimously.

Much attention to detail was necessary to organise a strike. Trade union law had to be rigorously followed. The Forest Gate team sent a member to all the workplaces to explain the dispute and gather support. The local MP attempted to approach the Chief to find a resolution but his efforts were short lived.

When the fateful day arrived every office and every court was picketed. Disruption was significant but did not attract any of the anticipated complaints. In the afternoon the MP and the only Black member of the team addressed a packed meeting in Forest Gate. Both speeches were impassioned and uplifting. Afterwards, as if respecting some tradition, the excited members drifted off to one or other of the local pubs.

Branch chair and secretary shook hands and walked away to their day jobs. For them the strike had represented failure not triumph.

Some years later the Chief retired. He had never seemed at peace with himself or anyone else and had managed during his tenure to unsettle and generally arouse. His rumbustious approach to everything paradoxically earned him a begrudging loyalty. His demands for high standards of client care were met without question. This was not a person who would have any truck with targets. He liked stories and would have enjoyed being the villain of this piece.

The Forest Gate team on being ejected from their building gradually dispersed. All will now have retired. They were a close knit group for that exciting time of innovation. In the years that followed each of them achieved distinction, whether in senior Probation or Health management, in academia or in film production. They were particularly respected for their creativity, imagination and willingness to take risks.

Mike Head

AQUATIC FUN

I was working in a youth team in a small town in South Wales. Paul, my colleague, and I had set up an 'activity group' in the local leisure centre.

We had about six to eight young people who attended regularly. Some of the group were quite difficult to handle in this type of setting but Paul and I were confident and experienced and had a good relationship with all of the members.

One of the girls, Queenie, had quite a reputation in the probation office for being difficult. Queenie was very overweight and was often perceived as being intimidating: she had severe mental health difficulties and was often volatile. She enjoyed the activity group, although on a previous occasion she had been found running around the leisure centre with a wooden pole and threatening staff: we were on our last warning at the centre.

It was summer and the weather was warm, so we decided to go swimming. Paul and I got there early and were already in the pool when the young people arrived. Queenie entered the pool area wearing a particularly tight swimming costume. She went straight for the helter skelter slide and started to climb the steps.

Paul and I rushed across the pool to wait at the bottom for her. As she came barreling down the slide towards us, both Paul and I realised in that moment that Queenie was not just over weight, but heavily pregnant. Paul and I looked anxiously at each other. After the session ended we had a chat with Queenie and took her to see the GP who confirmed our suspicions.

Queenie gave birth some four days later.

We visited her in hospital. Sadly, her baby was taken into care.

Alyson Rees

THE FAMOUS TIE SKETCH

The year: 1978.

On the first morning attention was drawn to the hat to be worn to court by women POs. Here, POs were still ' Servants of the Court'. 'Could you please open that window Mr....?' Later of course POs were to become 'Officers of the Court' – not sure the distinction was either accurate or made a scrap of difference. Whilst then in Essex there was crime in abundance this was an upwardly mobile population happy with their escape from East London, and understandably aspiring. For a young PO though the struggle to introduce fresh thinking, never mind a political dimension, was a tiresome and largely unproductive experience.

Nothing however could have prepared anyone for joining the North East London Service. No hats for Court here, but wardrobe and dress sense is at the heart of the emerging story.

Saturday Night Fever and Wales winning the 5 Nations plus the Grand Slam, with the immortal *Gareth Edwards and Phil Bennett.* More broadly and for those who demand social context the dominant image would be of industrial unrest, states of emergency and general chaos. What had taken place a decade earlier shaped the times. Loss of Empire, beginnings of de-industrialisation, more women working, mass immigration, destruction of familiar urban environment, social liberalism, youth culture and the rise of higher education - the glorious '60s.

Where was Probation in all of this change? Well, lagging behind might be one way of describing the slow pace of adjustment. A more contemporary view might be that what we had then was vastly better than what we have now.

With POs and the Chief seeing eye to eye about how probation should work the natural order of dispute between employer and employee had to take a different direction. An early battle concerned the texture of toilet paper. Following that victory they were as if in retaliation faced with criticism about dress code. Well this was 1978 not 1928; jeans and dungarees were not casual rather a uniform – a signal perhaps to clients of a willingness to engage on their terms rather than emphasising difference through the formal attire of suits and skirts.

Out of the blue reprised the 'You are Servants of the Courts' belief. The Secretary of the Probation Committee instructed that Warrant Cards would only be issued where male POs were, in the identifying photograph, wearing a tie. Well in Waltham Forest there was always a spare tie knocking about in case of that unexpected dash into Court. The implication of the tie wearing instruction however was that male POs should never be seen tieless.

Now as with the toilet paper caper you might think quarrelling about a tie to be frivolous in the extreme. However, the issue was seen then as a metaphor concerning misplaced and out-dated power and control.

The Chief would not have been unaware of the stirrings of dress code discontent, indeed he might have welcomed the opportunity to share with the staff he managed his own despair about the Probation Committee. Privately he had nick-names for the more active members and he had a particular dislike of the Chair of the time, who when not being a Magistrate was a local property dealer. Moreover the Chief would have noticed the hypocrisy when the Chair who was pursuing the dress code campaign with some vigour, was himself turning up for committee meetings wearing an ageing cardigan over a string vest.

So we move now to the spring of 1979 and the North East London Annual Conference. The Chief was taking a risk inviting each workplace unit to demonstrate by whatever means an illustration of their current preoccupations.

'A*nd........ we turn now to Waltham Forest*.......'

Some shuffling of chairs with the entire staff group of men and woman taking to the stage all wearing ties conspicuous by their colour, length and style. Gentle murmurings of amusement, a quiet uncertainty of what would happen next. Several of the Waltham Forest team then morphed into a representation of the Probation Committee, seemingly interviewing applicants for POs positions. But….judging the applicants solely by the quality of their respective ties. Qualifications and experience were ignored. The ties alone mattered. Having selected the applicant with the gaudiest tie the committee high stepped it off, stage left, to a recording of "Puttin' On The Ritz".

Then, with a very large pair of scissors a member of the team ceremoniously one by one cut each tie in half. There was a silence as the audience looked on at the absurd sight of twenty of their colleagues quietly clueless but at least appropriately dressed. The Chief described the whole thing as being frivolous. Notwithstanding in the years that followed it became known as the 'Famous Tie Sketch'.

Ilid Davies

SATURDAY COURT DUTY REASSESSED

{This article is, of course, fictitious… It was
written in the 1980s.)

For decades now the Probation Officer has been a loyal, dedicated servant of the court, assisting the bench by preparing reports and offering themselves as a buffer between the often confused and distressed defendant and the seemingly inexplicable and hostile machinations of the criminal justice system. We have carried out this task in a manner that is highly professional, skilful and valuable to all concerned. We are rightly proud of the status we have achieved as officers of the court who have always made the interests of the defendant our primary concern. Always, that is, except on a Saturday.

On a Saturday none of the above is at all relevant. On a Saturday different considerations come to the fore. The only principle which operates on a Saturday is that of getting home as soon as possible, without doing any work at all.

The best way of getting home as soon as possible, of course, is never to leave home at all. This is achieved by forgetting that you were ever meant to be on court duty that Saturday. Our advice is that this can be achieved two or three times in your entire career. As this requires trading on an otherwise impeccable professional reputation, and nerves of steel, it is not a course of action recommended for a first year officer. The appropriate attitude to adopt on your return to normal work on a Monday is difficult to acquire and there may be benefits in rehearsing at home in front of a mirror. Every act and word must betray your utter distress and shame; no amount of consolation and kindness from your colleagues could begin to rescue you from the abyss of grief and guilt into which you have fallen. Spend several hours publicly composing a suicidally apologetic letter to the Magistrate and Clerk. Make totally unrealistic offers of recompense to the court and your colleagues until they are beginning to become bored and irritated by your response to the whole episode.

If you have actually turned up at court the following have proved useful strategies in furthering the aim of getting home as soon as possible without doing any work.

The invisible probation officer: the next best thing to not being at court is for no one at court to know that you are there. The invisible probation officer blends into the decor of the court so completely as to become a barely noticed part of the furniture. Your clothing is very important here.

Dark oak trad court:

Men: brown suit (or possibly tweed). Small check if nothing else available. Plain shirt in neutral colours. Quiet tie.

Women: Laura Ashley autumn shades (never spring greens or blues). No make up (if you can handle it). 30 denier tights (compulsory).

(B) Bright 'high tech' court

Men: sober sports jacket, light grey trousers. Hush Puppies.

Women: corduroy skirt, brushed cotton or Viyella top. Sensible Brogues.

Be in court before the magistrates. Never draw attention to yourself by making a late entrance or leaving court while it is sitting. Avoid giving your name to the court usher. If successful, you could go through the whole morning without being used. You know that you are well on your way to becoming an invisible probation officer if the magistrate says "Can the probation service help?" and you are able to turn around and look for the probation officer with everyone else.

The perpetual motion privation officer: If your true identity has been revealed, the usher has got your name, or you are inappropriately dressed for Saturday court duty, you must then have to adopt the guise of the perpetual motion probation officer. This is a difficult technique to perfect but well worth persevering with as the benefits can be enormous. The key to this strategy is to keep moving at all times. The basic equipment needed is a file under the arm, pen in opposite hand, harassed expression on the face. It is essential here to enter court after the magistrate, giving the impression of having just interviewed the entire waiting room beforehand. Pause, then look directly at the magistrate as if pleading for no more extra work from the bench. Then walk briskly towards the cells, giving the impression that you are now going to interview everyone else there too. However, do not be tempted to linger there (or even go to the cells), but instead walk back into the waiting area, remaining out of sight for that length of time it would take you to interview four people on a weekday. (Make sure there are actually people in custody.) Return to court and repeat the process until court rises.

If, in spite of the above, you have been revealed as a probation officer, and the magistrate is beginning to use you as if it were a weekday, you have to develop an illness of such obvious severity that no magistrate with an ounce of humanity could possibly require your further attendance at court. This will be particularly necessary if you see a time-consuming case looming further down the court list. The following have been known to lead to a rapid deterioration in the health of a Saturday court duty officer:

bail hostel requests.

juveniles. (You may be left with them at the end of court).

defendants obviously under the influence of drink or drugs.

The homeless.

Anyone with an address not within reasonable travelling distance of your court who may want to go back there.

Anyone in tears or with an obvious problem.

Anyone with a pushchair.

Anyone behaving strangely.

People without shoes.

Saturday is a lovely day. Saturday is a day for gently nursing hangovers. Saturday is a day for staying in bed. Saturday is a day for that extra slice of toast, for reading the paper in bed, for watching telly, for being with your loved ones, for religious observances or for spending money, but not for spending the morning in court. So should any hint of guilt creep in while you are trying to blend into the court surroundings, whizzing around the court room or feigning a violent attack of distemper, remember that Saturday court duty is unnatural and inhumane, and think of how you would normally be spending your time in a more just and equitable society where such outrages were not permitted to happen.

Kevin Kirwin and Denise Shefras